The RESET WORKBOOK

* * * * *

A GUIDE TO FINDING YOUR INNER MAGIC

SPRUCE BOOKS
A Sasquatch Books Imprint

Printed in China

SPRUCE BOOKS with colophon is a registered
trademark of Penguin Random House LLC

27 26 25 24 23   9 8 7 6 5 4 3 2 1

Editor: Sharyn Rosart, Hannah Elnan
Production editor: Isabella Hardie
Designer: Alison Keefe

ISBN: 978-1-63217-476-5

Spruce Books, a Sasquatch Books Imprint

1325 Fourth Avenue, Suite 1025
Seattle, WA 98101

SasquatchBooks.com

FSC
www.fsc.org

MIX
Paper from
responsible sources
FSC® C188448

This book is dedicated to

my mom, my sister, my beautiful niece, my big bro,
my grandma, the aunties, my cousins. . .

and all the incredible people that walked with me
in this wacky adventure we call life.

THANK YOU!

CONTENTS

IT'S TIME FOR A RESET IF...
YOU'RE ALWAYS TIRED.
YOU FEEL OUT OF SYNC.
YOU'RE LIVING ON AUTOPILOT.
YOU FEEL DISCONNECTED.
YOU'RE READY FOR CHANGE.

You're probably wondering . . . is this book really for me? Maybe you're thinking: My life is pretty good. I like this. I love that. This is working okay.

But I bet your mind also flashed over to that one area of your life you don't let yourself dwell on too much. The part that's slightly out of sync, but that also will take some dedicated effort to make a meaningful change.

You probably know that even a single small tweak, one tiny optimization, could make you at least 3 percent happier. Now think about how over the course of doing this workbook, you'll find lots of tiny things to tweak. And that's how 3 percent happier becomes 30 percent happier.

Your life doesn't have to be in shambles to need a reset.

In fact, regularly checking in with yourself and making sure you're on the right track, or doing a little course correction if necessary, is essential for living the life you want.

It may seem like an unexamined life is easier, but such a life is full of missed opportunities—and it's a lot more boring.

This book will probably change your life. Though maybe not in the ways you expect.

I've had my fair share of resets.

There was the time I left my safe and secure full-time job to open a graphic design studio.

There was a beautiful relationship that changed my life trajectory.

And five years later, the breakup that changed my life trajectory again.

There was the decision to close down my design studio and become a creative director for a social media agency.

There was the decision to go to therapy. The decision to start working out regularly. To practice meditation. To eat healthier.

Launching a weekly wellness newsletter.

The move to a new city where I knew no one and starting over from scratch.

Making new friends. Losing old friends. Reconnecting with the most unexpected people.

There was a pandemic.

And the career pivot from advertising to tech. From creative director to director of marketing.

There was self-publishing a book.

And once again, quitting my safe and secure full-time job to chase my dream of being a full-time creator.

There were years that I pushed.

There were years when I waited.

There were storms.
False starts.
Confusing conversations.
And frustrating situations.

But I navigated them all with faith, passion, and purpose.

And that brings us to now.

Me living my beautiful, messy life. Where I draw and write and learn and teach.

And let me be clear: it's not perfect.

There are awesome moments and not-so-awesome moments.

But I designed this life, and on the days when I am uninspired, I feel empowered to adapt, grow, and change.

That's the beauty of *The Reset Workbook*.

Every time I sense that it's time for a meaningful life change, I work through these prompts again—and every time, it makes my life better.

CHANGE IS SCARY
CHANGE IS CONFUSING
CHANGE IS HARD.

BUT OFTENTIMES A
LITTLE DISCOMFORT
LEADS TO INCREDIBLE
GROWTH.

Between busy work days and demanding social lives, many of us don't make time to check in on our goals. We need an easy way to stay accountable.

I've developed a process for making a plan to get what you want. It's straightforward—and also pretty fun.

The Reset Workbook is designed in a way that invites you to physically interact with your goals by writing about them. It offers lots of personal analysis, opportunities for brainstorming, and inspirational quotes. The primary goal, however, is to build a tactical roadmap to make your dreams a reality. Here's how it works.

You:

- Answer questions

- Brainstorm potential goals

- Narrow them down

- Set intentions for the next year

Remember: this is a living document meant to be examined regularly, and altered to fit your ever-changing version of a fulfilling, meaningful life.

The workbook is separated into specific categories to help you navigate the most vital parts of your personal identity. You'll learn more about yourself and have the tools to design a path that makes you happier and healthier.

Get ready to be pulled and stretched in magical ways.

Write, color, scribble, but most importantly, enjoy!

This workbook is organized into ten chapters of change. In each one, you'll reflect on an area of your life to help you better define your vision for the future.

MIND P. 19

Learn how to manage your thoughts and treat yourself to the loving-kindness you deserve.

PURPOSE P. 33

Define your values, mission, and passions, so you can connect with your purpose right now.

BODY P. 51

Discover how to think positively about your body and celebrate the beauty that you carry with you every single day.

SELF-CARE P. 71

Promote your emotional, physical, mental, and spiritual well-being with healthy habits.

SPIRIT P. 83

Look beyond the physical realm and dive deeper into your universal truths to light your soul on fire.

01

START HERE

The average person makes about 35,000 decisions on any given day. What do I wear? Where do I park? What should I cook for dinner?

This usually means that by the time you get home from work, you're tired of thinking, and more likely to veg out in front of the TV than to invest time in making your dreams a reality.

That's why it's vital to make time to check in with yourself. Choose a time and put it in your calendar. You're going to focus on you and what moves you.

The following section will ask big and small questions to help you figure out where you are and decide what truly matters to you. If you can pair your passions with a strategic focus, you'll find it easier to keep your life in alignment.

TEMPERATURE CHECK

Rate how you're feeling in each area from a 1–10, where 1 is the lowest and 10 is the highest.

SCORE 1–10	AREA OF YOUR LIFE
	My sense of self
	My general enjoyment with my career
	My relationships with friends and family
	My connection with my body
	My use of free time
	My spiritual experiences
	My vacation time
	My sex life
	My hobbies and personal development

YOU CAN LET
LIFE HAPPEN
TO YOU

OR YOU CAN BUILD
A LIFE YOU ACTUALLY
KINDA LIKE.

ALWAYS CHANGING

One thing I learned about myself over the past three months:

I'm happy because this happened:

This quarter led me to:

I'm happy this ended in the past three months:

EVERYTHING IS
So CONFUSING,
BUT SOMEHOW
I'M STILL SMILING.

TOP FIVE MOMENTS

What beautiful things happened in the last three months?

01

02

03

04

05

USEFUL ADVICE

If I could go back in time, what advice would I give myself?

01

02

03

04

05

06

07

08

09

10

DON'T CHASE HAPPINESS.
HAPPINESS ISN'T A GOAL;
IT'S A BY-PRODUCT OF
A WELL-DESIGNED LIFE.

CHASE PURPOSE.
PURPOSE KEEPS
YOU GROWING.

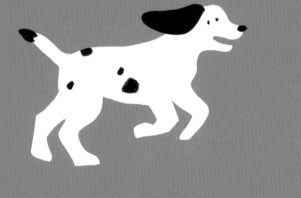

THINGS THAT ENERGIZE ME

01

02

03

04

05

SO THANKFUL

Ten things I'm thankful for, including people, moments, experiences, and things:

01

02

03

04

05

06

_____

07

_____

08

_____

09

_____

10

YOUR TRANSFORMATION HAS
A COST. TO BE REBORN, A
CERTAIN VERSION OF YOU
HAS TO DIE... AND THAT'S
SO BEAUTIFUL.

THINGS THAT MAKE ME FEEL EXHAUSTED

01

02

03

04

05

WANTS

What are five things that I want to add to my life right now?

01

02

03

04

05

COMMUNITY

GRATITUDE

MINDFULNESS

JOY

SELF-AWARENESS

SIMPLICITY

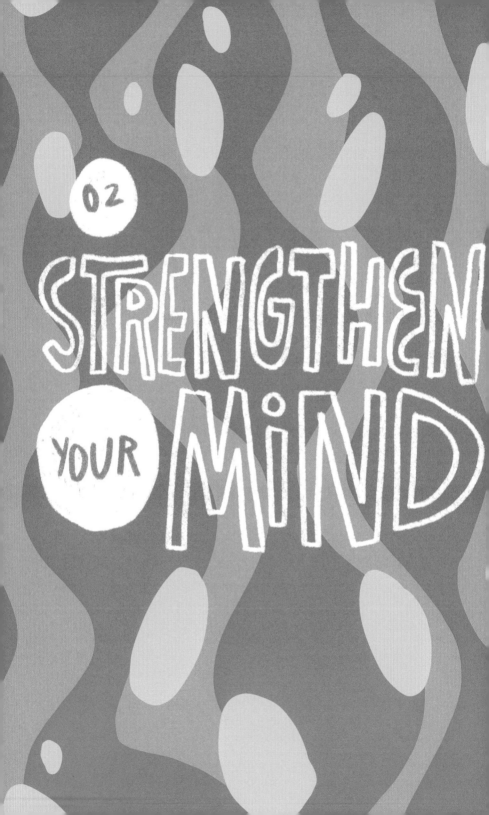

The human brain is a beautiful thing. But for many, it can also be a breeding ground for negative thoughts.

Three pounds. 100 billion neurons. The capability of generating 23 watts of power.

While you can't control all of your circumstances, you can always control how you respond to a situation. It all starts with your thoughts.

Imagine your story the way you want it to be.

Your mind is your most valuable resource, and it's the primary thing that gives you the confidence and power to succeed.

In this section, we'll focus on the best ways to manage negative thoughts and consistently fill your brain with the loving-kindness it deserves.

HOW TO COMBAT NEGATIVE SELF-TALK

1. WRITE DOWN YOUR FEELINGS.

The process of putting your feelings into written form helps you to understand and process your emotions. Once you've put it all down on the page, you may find a little emotional distance, which makes it easier to see how these negative notions might not be totally true. To further allow yourself to let go, challenge each negative thought with a positive one that directly reframes the thought you originally wrote.

2. TRY TO LIVE IN THE PRESENT.

Instead of rehashing the past or stressing over the future, try to stay in this moment. Mindfulness is a useful tool to get you out of a thought spiral and back into the current moment. The simplest way to do it is to focus on your breath. Breathe in and out slowly; concentrate on the physical sensations happening in your body.

3. MOVE YOUR BODY.

Physical activity is a 100 percent positive way to distract from negative thoughts. Even ten minutes of aerobic exercise or lifting weights can reset your mood and reoxygenate your blood, helping you to think more clearly and positively. Turn on music and dance around the house! Or do yoga to breathe through a pose and gain new perspective.

4. MAKE ROOM FOR GRAY AREAS.

No situation is all bad or all good. Often, negative self-talk is framed in extremes, as in "I'm never going to find someone to love!" or "I'm going to get fired from my job and lose everything!" In reality, life is never just black and white. Instead of jumping to big conclusions, allow yourself the space to pause and reflect and find nuance in your situation. This will help you focus on more realistic outcomes instead.

5. LIMIT NEGATIVITY IN YOUR LIFE.

This might mean unfollowing certain people on social media or not watching the news the first thing in the morning. It could mean avoiding people who are energy vampires. By removing obvious sources of negativity in your life, you make more room for positive thinking.

6. USE POSITIVE AFFIRMATIONS.

A lot of times negative thinking comes from low self-esteem. One of the best ways to build self-esteem is to repeat positive affirmations. While it might feel awkward at first, giving yourself positive affirmations can help unravel negative thought patterns in your life, creating new pathways in your brain. Repeating the phrases helps to rewrite your story and ultimately encourages you to make positive changes in your life.

7. PRACTICE FEELING GRATEFUL.

Make time to celebrate all of the wonderful things that have happened or how far you've actually come. The daily practice of writing down things that you're grateful for can be life-changing. Staying in a mindset of gratitude can turn off the tendency to feel sad and defeated. Gratitude can help you believe that the storms you face are actually strength training for the life you ultimately want to lead.

8. TALK TO YOURSELF LIKE YOU'RE A CHILD.

Negative self-talk typically shows up when we've made a mistake. But mistakes are normal and everyone makes them. Parent your inner child by gently nudging yourself in the right direction as if you're talking to a three-year-old. Learn to lead with love—especially when you're talking to yourself.

WHAT'S HOLDING ME BACK?

NAME THE FEAR	HOW CAN I MANAGE THE FEAR?

I KNOW IT MIGHT NOT FEEL LIKE IT, BUT YOU ARE LOVED, EVEN IN YOUR LONELIEST MOMENTS.

PROFESSIONAL STRENGTHS

01

02

03

04

05

PERSONAL GIFTS & STRENGTHS

01

02

03

04

05

MY GROWTH AREAS

01

02

03

04

05

DEFINING ME

What is the title of this next chapter in my life?

What do I wish I had more time to do?

When do I feel the most like myself?

What is something I love learning about?

LEARNING
TO BE MORE
HONEST WITH
MYSELF

UNHELPFUL MENTAL HABITS

01

02

03

04

05

There's no manual for life, but there are some indisputable truths.

You have a unique set of gifts and the ability to develop new skills.

It's your responsibility to cultivate those gifts and skills and share them, because the world desperately needs the uncommon magic you were born to create.

That's the heart of your purpose.

Your gifts. Your skills. Your passions. Your values. And figuring out how you can use them to make an impact in the world.

It's a big-picture conceptual idea, but the end result is usually simple.

HOW TO DEFINE YOUR VALUES

Your values are the guiding principles—the things you believe deep inside that help you navigate decision-making.

Whether consciously or unconsciously, we all have internal metrics that let us know if we feel like our life is on track and has meaning. To better connect with that inner feeling, you can establish your own framework for decision-making.

Choose ten words from the list below that resonate with you, or brainstorm your own.

Achievement	Humility	Stability
Adventure	Humor	Status
Attention to Detail	Integrity	Success
Authenticity	Justice	Tolerance
Balance	Kindness	Trustworthiness
Beauty	Leadership	Wealth
Boldness	Learning	Wisdom
Community	Love	_____
Compassion	Loyalty	_____
Courage	Openness	_____
Creativity	Optimism	_____
Curiosity	Peace	_____
Determination	Poise	_____
Empathy	Power	_____
Faith	Reputation	_____
Fame	Resilience	_____
Family	Responsibility	_____
Freedom	Security	_____
Friendships	Self-Reliance	_____
Generosity	Self-Respect	_____
Growth	Selflessness	_____
Helping Others	Service	_____
Honesty	Spirituality	_____

MY VALUES

01

02

03

04

05

AFFIRMING MY VALUES

Are my top five values an accurate reflection of who I am right now? Why or why not?

Do the people I spend the most time with exemplify the values on my list?

How can I remind myself to uphold these values in my daily life?

4 COMMON MISCONCEPTIONS ABOUT FINDING YOUR PURPOSE

Finding your purpose is meaningful work we should all strive to accomplish, but it can feel daunting. Here are a few common misconceptions that might be holding you back from stepping into your power:

You have just one purpose in your life.

Not exactly. Over the course of your life, you change, evolve, and grow. With these changes, your purpose will also change. So be flexible with yourself and choose to accept where you are, but also to embrace where you want to go.

Here's the thing: you can't compare your calling to someone else's. Your purpose is shaped to fit you right where you are, right now. Maybe it's something monumental that changes the world. But it's also totally okay (and more likely) that your purpose affects only your immediate family or surroundings. The world needs both. Big and small are equally important—a small act may have consequences, while a seemingly major one might cause only a minor ripple.

Their purpose is more important than my purpose.

The best way to find your purpose is to wait.

While sometimes life will call for you to be patient and wait, usually the best way to find your purpose is to commit to action. Trying new things and testing new ideas is a great way to figure out what you actually love doing. Your purpose is almost always found in the things that you naturally gravitate toward.

Unfortunately, no. Finding and following your purpose does not mean that you will be happy 100 percent of the time. Navigating challenges is a regular part of life for all people. There will always be good and bad days. But having a clearly defined purpose will bring meaning, joy, and peace to your days of living in this complicated world.

Finding your purpose will lead to your happily ever after.

DISCOVERING MY PURPOSE

What do I love doing? From childhood to today, what could I get lost in and do for hours?

What skills do I admire in other people?

What am I passionate about outside of work?

What skills do I have that can earn money?

What am I naturally gifted at doing?

In what situations do I feel the most at ease?

HOW TO FIND YOUR PURPOSE

Embrace your curiosity and continue learning.

Whether you loved school or not, life is a form of continuing education. There are so many beautiful things to learn in this world. New skills. New frameworks. New ideas. Embrace your inner child and always investigate the world with fresh eyes.

Heal from the pain you've experienced.

We all have things that happened in our lives that hurt, things that make us sad. Challenges we wish we never had to endure. But until you confront those things, they will continue to guide your story. Working through these areas and talking about them with a trained professional can be the key to moving forward and charting a new path.

Find and nurture your community.

Developing meaningful relationships as an adult is hard, but each of us was born to live in relationships with other people. The only way to have meaningful relationships is to tap into your vulnerability and put yourself out there. Once you've found your people, show up for them. Be a sincere listener, a kind friend, and a willing participant in their growth and development.

Look inward and reflect.

Understanding yourself is an essential step toward finding and living in your purpose. The good news is that if you're reading this, then you're well on your way to doing the work necessary to establish your purpose. Continue to write, journal, read, and reflect. These activities will continue to guide you toward the person you want to become.

This graphic reflects the Japanese concept of *ikigai* or "reason for being." The overlap in your passion, mission, vocation, and profession represents your purpose.

WHAT YOU LOVE DOING

PASSION

MISSION

WHAT YOU'RE GOOD AT

WHAT THE WORLD NEEDS

PROFESSION

VOCATION

WHAT YOU CAN BE PAID FOR

GETTING SPECIFIC

What's my passion?

What's my mission?

What's my ideal profession?

What's my vocation?

EXAMPLES OF PURPOSE STATEMENTS

My purpose is to use my problem-solving skills to make a significant change in the world.

My purpose is to bring joy everywhere I go.

My purpose is to turn ideas into reality.

My purpose is to pour as much love as I can into the world.

My purpose in this season is to create art consistently.

My purpose is to be a source of peace for my family.

My purpose is to facilitate meaningful connections between the people I encounter.

My purpose is to expose as many parents as possible to the power of therapy for kids.

My purpose in life is to write stories about the Latinx experience that connect with people's hearts and minds.

My purpose is to encourage other women to start their own businesses.

My purpose is to give my children a safe and loving home and set them up for future success.

My purpose is to defend the rights of all people and create equality in my workplace.

My purpose in this season is to live life to the fullest and continually have new experiences.

FIND YOUR PURPOSE

We're all here for a specific reason, with something to give, a way to make meaning. What are four ideas for my purpose?

01

02

03

04

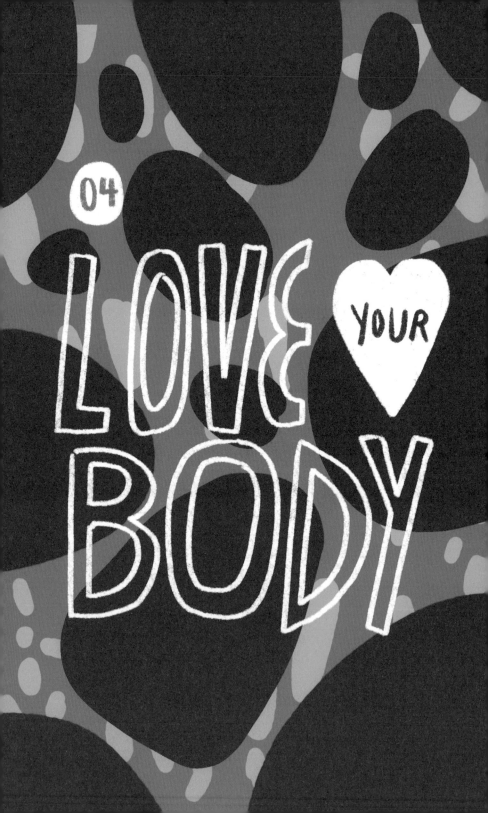

Your body is your connection with the world.

It's also the vessel that holds your marvelous spirit.

Your body is something to love and cherish, to take care of daily, to nourish with good food, to strengthen with regular and joyful movement, and to maintain with conscientious self-care.

But for so many of us, our bodies are a source of so much insecurity and shame.

This section is dedicated to learning how to think positively about your body; it is a space to celebrate the beauty you carry with you every day.

Remember: It's important to use positive words that are affirming. In this section, please be kind to yourself.

If you suspect you may be engaging in disordered eating, talk to your doctor or a mental health professional. Visit www. NationalEatingDisorders.org to learn more.

I AM BEAUTIFUL

How do I define beauty?

List three people I find beautiful. What do I find beautiful about them?

How has social media changed the way I think about beauty?

I feel most attractive when. . .

What's something that made me feel beautiful in the last three months?

What's the most common compliment I receive from people?

FRIENDLY REMINDER:

IT'S OK TO FEEL

UNDERSTANDING BODY IMAGE

Growing up, how did I feel about my body?

When was the first time I remember being judgmental of my body?

What have I denied myself because my body isn't perfect?

LOVING MY BEAUTIFUL BODY

What body image struggles am I going through right now?

How can I let go of any negative feelings I have about my body?

What does positive body image look like for me?

10 REASONS I'M THANKFUL FOR MY BODY

ACCEPTING MY BODY

What does body acceptance mean to me?

When I think of my body, what's the first word that comes to mind? Why?

What part of my body do I respect the most?

What's something positive I can say about my body?

Here's a list of reasons why I'm grateful for my body as it is:

Right now, my body needs:

LOVING MYSELF MORE

What would the world look like if no one had low body confidence?

To me, a beautiful person is:

When was the last time I felt comfortable in my body?

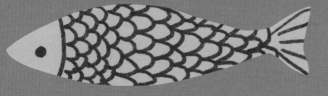

FIND YOUR OWN UNIQUE
AND BEAUTIFUL PATH

CONSCIOUSLY CONSUMING

What food makes me feel the most energized?

What's a new food or recipe I would like to try?

What's my go-to feel-good meal?

What should I consume less of to feel better?

_____

How mindful am I when I eat?

_____

What would I like to prioritize eating in the next three months?

TAKING CARE OF MY BODY

What advice would I give to someone else about loving their body more?

What's one small thing I can do today to feel better about my body?

How will I keep my body in motion over the next three months?

THE WORLD
NEEDS YOU
AND ALL OF
YOUR MAGIC.

DEFINING MY STYLE

One of the most beautiful forms of self-expression is the way that we present ourselves to the world. We each have unique ways that we choose to adorn ourselves.

Your personal style is a story that your share with the world daily. On the next page, circle the words that most connect with the way you want to be perceived in the world. Then use those words to create a description of your personal style.

Bohemian	Effortless	Sleek
Bold	Elegant	Sporty
Calming	Elevated	Statement-Making
Cheerful	Experimental	Structural
Classic	Minimalistic	Sultry
Clean	Polished	Tailored
Colorful	Preppy	Timeless
Comfortable	Quirky	Trendy
Confident	Refined	Tropical
Cool	Relaxed	Understated
Downtown	Romantic	Vintage
Edgy	Simple	Whimsical

Using any of the words above, or words of my own, here's how I would define my personal style:

STYLE ADVICE

Three people whose style I admire and why:

Who are my style heroes?

What's my favorite place to shop? How would I describe the vibe?

What pieces do I need to add to my wardrobe?

What specific clothing items do I wear the most? Why?

What do I want to remove from my wardrobe to feel more like me?

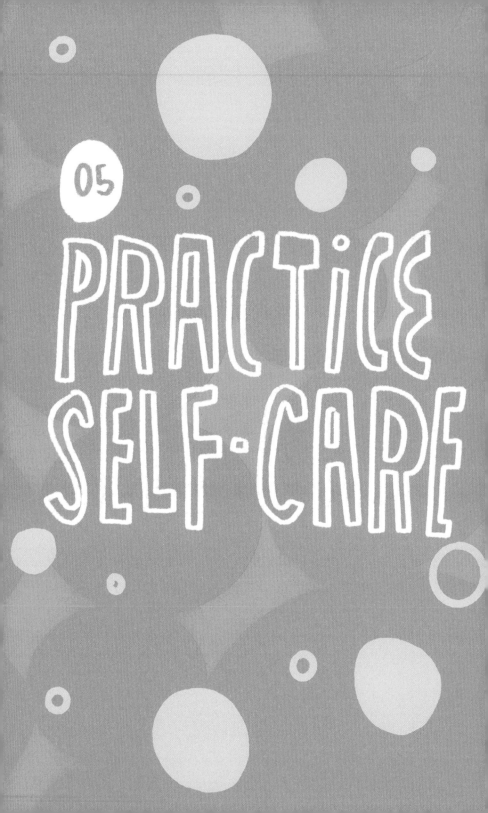

05

PRACTICE
SELF·CARE

Self-care isn't just about bubble baths, facials, shopping sprees, and other forms of indulgence.

Self-care is any activity that we consciously do to promote our emotional, physical, mental, and/or spiritual well-being.

It's listening to yourself and honoring your true needs.

Self-care is regularly moving your body. Making healthy meals. Scheduling doctor's appointments. Creating boundaries in relationships. Taking time to enjoy nature. Listening to music that makes you happy. Appreciating the things and people you are grateful for.

Contrary to popular belief, self-care is not selfish. Self-care often requires lots of discipline.

In this section you'll think about stress, rest, and healthy coping mechanisms for building a healthier life for yourself.

DEALING WITH STRESS

On a scale from 1–10, what level is my anxiety right now? What's causing me to be anxious?

What contributes the most to my stress? Is there anything I can do to change that?

How does stress affect my daily life?

WRITE DOWN EVERYTHING YOU'RE WORRIED ABOUT.

MANAGING STRESS

How do I currently manage stress?

What's one small step I can take to feel more relaxed?

What helps me calm down when I feel overwhelmed?

LEARNING TO RELAX

When do I feel the most calm and relaxed? How can I create more of that feeling?

What helps me feel supported in challenging times?

What is a past challenge that ended up being a source of growth?

SELF-CARE IDEAS

STAY
HYDRATED

MAKE A
SCHEDULE

JOURNAL

RELAXING
BATHS

PLAY WITH
YOUR PET

QUALITY
SLEEP

LISTEN TO
MUSIC

REGULAR
WORKOUTS

HEALTHY
MEALS

SELF-CARE

Finish this sentence: I take care of myself by. . .

Where do I go for peace and quiet?

What hobby helps me relax?

UNDERSTANDING MY SLEEP

How long does it generally take me to fall asleep at night?

When I get a great night's rest, how do I feel? What about after a bad night?

Do I usually sleep through the night? If not, why do I wake up? Can I go back to sleep?

Do my thoughts race at bedtime? What can I do to alleviate some of this nighttime anxiety?

How much caffeine do I have in a typical day?

Is there something I know is causing sleep problems for me?

RESTFUL MINDSET

What's one small thing I can do to improve my sleep?

How can I create a bedroom that is relaxing and promotes good sleep?

Can I stop looking at screens at least an hour before bed? What can I do instead?

Ideas for a relaxing bedtime routine:

MAKING ROOM
FOR THE REST
I NEED

06

EMBRACE
SPIRIT

Spirituality is the part of us that senses there is something greater than ourselves.

Something more than the sum of its parts, that connects us to all living things.

And cultivating your spirit is a way to connect with the most profound truths of life, those that go beyond our egos and our daily concerns to a place of deeper meaning.

This section is designed to check in on your spiritual life and help you take steps to nourish your spiritual growth.

Regardless of your background or beliefs, the goal is to give yourself the freedom to think outside the body and mind and go deeper into universal truths.

You can do this in so many ways, including through studying philosophy, practicing religion, meditating, engaging in service work, or through a deep appreciation of nature.

Embracing your spirituality is an opportunity to feel connected to a great oneness, to be thankful for the universe, our planet, other human beings, and all the majestic creatures that inhabit our world.

FINDING SPIRITUALITY

What does spirituality mean to me?

What parts of spirituality do I reject or retain from my childhood?

What do I believe makes the world a better place?

How would I describe my relationship with a higher power?

Do I see myself as a good person? Why or why not?

Are there any spiritual practices I would like to learn more about?

LIFE AND DEATH

What do I think happens when people die?

What do I want to be remembered for after I die?

What makes me feel the most alive?

MY HIGHEST SELF

How do I describe my highest, best self?

One thing I've learned on my spiritual journey so far:

What practices nurture my spiritual self?

EXPLORING CONNECTION

How can I connect more with nature?

How do I want to explore my connection to the universe in the next three months?

What does it mean to be connected to the world around me?

PRACTICE EMOTIONAL INTELLIGENCE

Over the course of the day, you experience hundreds of thoughts and countless feelings.

You shift between different moods. Some fleeting. Some lasting a long time.

And everyone you encounter is living in their own experiences. Processing their own challenges. Doing the best they can in a confusing world.

Emotional intelligence is the ability to understand and manage emotions. It doesn't always come naturally.

It's a set of skills to be learned by living life with an open heart, a positive mindset, and the internal motivation to self-regulate our responses to intense emotions—and the willingness to notice and care about other people's feelings.

This section offers opportunities to understand your emotions better and harness your power to spread love in the world.

HOW AM I FEELING?

How much power do daily circumstances have over me? How do I normally respond to inconveniences?

What emotions am I trying to avoid right now? What's standing in the way of being able to address this feeling?

How do I process strong feelings? Am I comfortable with intense emotions?

COMPLICATED EMOTIONS

When was the last time I felt envious of someone else? Why did I feel this way? How did I handle the situation?

Think about a time where I lost something or someone. What did I learn from that experience?

Who do I feel the most comfortable around in my life? Why?

TRANSFORMATION
IS ALWAYS
POSSIBLE.

EMOTIONAL RELEASE

Who or what makes me the most angry? How does that anger show up in my life? How can I manage it?

01

02

03

SHARE THE LIGHT

Four people who have brought me joy in the last three months, and a short message of thanks to each one.

01

02

03

04

TOGETHER WE FLOURISH.

QUOTABLE

There are moments where things don't go my way, moments where I feel totally unmotivated, moments when I feel lost. Here are my favorite quotes when I need inspiration.

01

02

03

04

YOUR IMPERFECTIONS DON'T MAKE YOU ANY LESS WORTH LOVING.

ALL THE FEELS

How do I handle anger and frustration?

Am I holding on to any regrets? How can I let my regrets go?

What emotion do I have difficulty expressing? Why is that?

When was the last time I cried? How often do I cry?

Are there barriers standing in the way of developing deeper relationships? How can I let those walls down?

What can I do to better manage my emotions?

TRUE CONNECTIONS

How happy am I in my most important personal relationships?

Do I seek approval from others? Why?

How often do I lose my temper? Is this something I want to change?

Are there relationships I would like to improve or deepen? How might
I do that?

HOW TO FEEL
MORE CONNECTED

LISTEN TO UNDERSTAND,
NOT TO RESPOND

MAINTAIN YOUR
SENSE OF HUMOR

SET HEALTHY
BOUNDARIES

ORGANIZE
REGULAR
FRIEND DATES

PRACTICE
EMPATHY

QUALITY CONNECTIONS

What connections have been the most powerful, and how are they sustaining me? What positive qualities do I bring to my relationships?

01

02

03

04

05

BUILDING RELATIONSHIPS

Who do I call in an emergency? Who can call on me in an emergency?

Is there someone in my life that I would be interested in getting to know better?

A person from my past I'd like to reconnect with and why:

FAMILY TIES

What's my relationship like with my parental figures? What works about these relationships? What doesn't work?

Who in my family do I depend on? How?

Which of my family relationships are working for me? What is my role in these relationships?

FRIENDSHIPS

What makes someone a good friend?

Am I a good friend? How can I be a better friend?

How do I show up for my friends when they need me?

BUILDING COMMUNITY
IS DIFFICULT WORK
THAT'S ABSOLUTELY
WORTH DOING.

08

ENJOY
WORK

On average, a third of our lives are spent working.

Now more than ever, many people are balancing a full-time job with at least some sort of part-time side hustle, either to make ends meet or to pursue a passion.

You deserve to do work you enjoy at least 80 percent of the time. But for most people, your career will not necessarily be your passion.

Instead, your career will be something that pays you a livable wage, and that you care about doing well. If you're lucky, it will also afford you the time to explore your interests outside of work and leave you enough time to spend with the people you love.

The purpose of this section is not to get you to quit your day job. It's to help you focus on building a career that offers meaning and a reasonable work/life balance.

MY CAREER NEEDS

What are non-negotiable needs I expect from work?

_____

01

_____

02

_____

03

_____

04

_____

05

06

07

08

09

10

HERE'S YOUR PERMISSION TO FIND JOY OUTSIDE OF WORK.

WORK HAPPY

What's a job I would absolutely never want to do again?

Why am I doing my current job?

If money weren't an issue, what would I do with my time?

CAREER GOALS

On a scale from 1–10, how would I rate the past three months of my job? Why?

What do I love about my current job?

What do I hate about my current job?

Are there any things I could do to make my current job more rewarding?

If I could have any other job, what would it be?

What are the qualities I want in my dream job?

MY ROLE MODELS

Who are three people I look to for career inspiration?

_____

01

_____

02

_____

03

THE PEOPLE
WE ADMIRE
REMIND US
TO LIVE
OUT LOUD.

MY WORKING STYLE

What does going above and beyond at work mean to me?

What's one solvable problem at work I'd like to personally tackle?

What's my work communication style?

On a scale from 1–10, how good am I at taking vacations? When can I schedule some time off?

What could I do better at work?

How do I deal with criticism at work? Is this something I want to change?

THE ONLY PERSON YOU'RE COMPETING WITH IS YOUR PAST SELF.

PICTURE OF SUCCESS

What's one lesson I learned from work in the past three months?

Who's my favorite person at work? Why do I like them so much?

Who do I admire at work? What qualities from them would I like to cultivate in myself?

IDEAL WORKDAY

Here's my ideal workday, hour by hour.

TIME	ACTIVITY

LOOKING TO MY FUTURE

A professional accomplishment I am proud of from the last three months:

What do I want my career to look like in the next five years?

Am I professionally fulfilled? What would that look like?

It's far too easy just to let life happen to you.

Here's a friendly reminder: You are the only one who can create the life you want to lead.

Just as you choose to guide your thoughts toward positivity, keep your relationships in good repair, and define a career that sustains you, you also get to create a lifestyle that you love.

Your home, your relationships, and your life outside of work. These elements are integral to defining your story.

This chapter is all about analyzing your current choices and adjusting them to give you the balance you deserve and the experiences that fulfill you.

HOME GOALS

What does my home currently say about me?

What do I like or love about my home right now? What is not working?

How do I want my home to feel when someone walks through the door?

_____

What colors am I most inspired by and want in my living space?

_____

What is one thing I would like to change about my home?

_____

Is there any space in my home that is underutilized? How can I update or optimize that space?

HOW TO FIND YOUR
DESIGN STYLE

1 DEFINE HOW YOU WANT YOUR SPACE TO FEEL.

2 LOOK AT YOUR FAVORITE CLOTHING ITEMS FOR INSPIRATION.

3 FIND YOUR INTERIOR DESIGN ROLE MODELS.

4 SOURCE COLOR PALETTES YOU LOVE.

5 BUILD A MOOD BOARD ON PINTEREST.

MY DESIGN STYLE

Whose interior design style am I inspired by?

What items in my home (or someone else's) do I absolutely love?

What items in my home should I get rid of?

THE MAGIC OF TINY TWEAKS

What's the easiest space for me to update quickly to make the most impact?

On a scale of 1–10 how messy/disorganized am I? How can I make my home more organized?

How do I feel about the artwork in my home? What would I love to see around me?

EASY WAYS TO UPDATE YOUR HOME

PAINT AN ACCENT WALL

GET A NEW RUG

BUY A PLANT

TRY A NEW LAMP

HANG CURTAINS

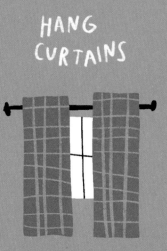

ADD THROW PILLOWS

JUST FOR FUN

Life should be more than just work. Here are ten things I would like to do just for fun, starting with what I want to try in the next three months.

01

02

03

04

05

06

07

08

09

10

DOWNTIME GOALS

Here's my perfect day off from start to finish. (Include some time for doing nothing much.)

TIME	ACTIVITY

FIND JOY BEING
AT REST.

BUILDING MY ITINERARY

What type of travel do I enjoy the most?

Travel advice I would give my younger self:

My next trip needs to make me feel:

TRAVEL GOALS

Places close to home for a quick weekend trip:

Places overseas or far away that would I like to visit:

If I could travel to only one country, it would be:

My top five bucket-list travel destinations:

A list of people I'd like to visit in the next three years:

My favorite travel companions:

TRAVEL BINGO

LOOKING BACK

One way that travel changed me:

My wildest travel story so far:

A place I would return to and why:

10

DEVELOP RITUALS

Rituals give meaning to our lives.

Whether they are built around a major occasion or just a mundane moment, rituals can create space for reflection, expression, or togetherness.

Something as simple as preparing a cup of tea and slowly savoring it while you read a magazine on a Sunday morning can add a sense of ritual to your experience.

You might play a specific set of songs on the drive into work to get you pumped up for the day. Or burn palo santo in your studio before working on a piece of art.

Maybe you call a parent or sibling every Sunday morning.

These repeated actions can add a unique value to your life. They can remind you to open your heart, give you the space to calm your spirit, or offer a chance to step outside your everyday challenges and create a special moment.

What daily, weekly, monthly, and quarterly rituals will you create?

MORNING RITUAL

My morning routine sets me up for a successful day. How do I want to begin my day? How are workdays and non-workdays different?

DAY	TIME	ACTIVITY

BUILD YOUR PERFECT MORNING

EXERCISE

MAKE A TO-DO LIST

DRINK TEA

MEDITATE

TAKE A WALK

PRAY

JOURNAL

READ A BOOK

NIGHTLY RITUAL

What can I do in the evening to set myself up for a restorative night?

DAY	TIME	ACTIVITY

DEVELOPING RITUALS

What's one small thing I can do every week to celebrate that I'm alive?

Is there a monthly ritual I would like to adopt to celebrate myself?

When am I holding my next personal retreat? Specifically, when and where is it?

EXPANDING MY RITUALS

What's my ritual for ending the workday and transitioning to my personal time in the evening?

What's my favorite holiday now? Why do I look forward to this holiday?

What's a small tradition I'd like to create with a friend or a small group? When would we do this ritual?

RITUALS to TRY

CALL MOM
ON TUESDAYS

10-MINUTE
DANCE PARTIES
TO RELIEVE STRESS

SUNDAY
BRUNCH

NO SCREENS
AFTER 8PM

BUY A NEW
OUTFIT FOR
JOB INTERVIEWS

KARAOKE
ONCE A
MONTH

MONTHLY
MOON
BATH

TINY RITUALS

What is my ritual for celebrating small wins?

What is my ritual for when I get stressed out at work?

How do I celebrate the end of a work week or a task well done?

MY PERSONAL HOLIDAYS

My list of set holidays I want to celebrate this year:

01

02

03

04

05

I IMAGINE THE PURPOSE
OF LIFE IS TO BECOME
THE PERSON I ALWAYS
KNEW I WAS.

BUILDING TRADITIONS

What's my favorite holiday memory from childhood? Why was this holiday so special?

What's a family tradition I'd like to carry on? Why is this tradition important to keep going?

What's a new family tradition I'd like to create for myself?

CELEBRATING LIFE

What's the best birthday celebration that I've had so far?

How would I like to celebrate my birthday this year?

What's a bucket-list birthday gift or experience I'd like to have?

YOU ARE SO IMPORTANT
AND SPECIAL, AND ALL
THAT LIGHT NEEDS
TO SHINE.

11

SET EPIC GOALS

Real talk: The average person has waaay too much going on.

Finding a healthy balance in work and personal life is a struggle for even the most disciplined. And honestly, we all have a little bit of procrastinator inside us.

However, there is a simple way to take deliberate action in creating good habits: setting goals.

There's power in setting a goal, watching yourself move toward it (and, let's be honest, sometimes away from it) over time, and ultimately crossing it off the list. Seeing this concrete progress builds self-esteem and sets you up to take on and succeed at even bigger goals.

HOW TO SET
EPIC GOALS

Go big and bold—but use a dash of realism.

The Reset Workbook is about stretching yourself, but also about setting goals you can realistically accomplish over the next year.

Find those tiny wins first, and as the months progress, aim bigger and brighter.

One of the most useful ways to make your goals realistic is to use my EPIC goals framework:

E — Essential
Is this absolutely necessary right now?

P — Purpose Driven
Does it align with the purpose I've established?

I — Identifiable
Can I easily identify what meeting the goal looks like?

C — Clearly Defined
Do I know exactly when to do it and for how long?

Now let's get practical. Instead of saying "I want to eat healthier," you would replace it with:

IDENTIFIABLE

"I will cook three times a week using fresh ingredients because slowing down to prepare healthy meals gives me joy."

CLEARLY DEFINED

PURPOSE DRIVEN

ESSENTIAL

What makes this an EPIC goal? Eating healthy is essential to the life you want to lead. It aligns with your purpose of treating yourself well, slowing down, and experiencing life's daily pleasures. It is easily identifiable because you know if you've done it, and it is clearly defined by a schedule.

By regularly checking in on your EPIC goals, you can also pivot whenever necessary. Goals are guideposts, but they're not set in stone and they can also frequently shift.

Perhaps after two months, you realize that cooking three times a week is unrealistic for your hectic work schedule. That's totally fine. You can always redefine your plan.

Maybe you refine your goals from cooking at home three times a week to doing it once a week, but choosing to eat out at vegetarian restaurants to make sure you're still eating healthier.

GOAL IDEAS

Here's a list of some of the most common goals to help kick-start your brainstorming session.

Exercise 2x per week

Practice cooking one of grandmother's recipes

Journal every day for a month

Train for and run a 5K, 10K, or marathon in the next 6 months

Make a scrapbook of my favorite travel adventures

Learn to play "Black Hole Sun" on the piano

Update resume or portfolio and apply for 10 new jobs

Take a class in conversational Japanese

Outline a novel in 90 days

Organize closet

Launch a new website for side business

Save enough money to go on a trip outside the country

Get a tattoo with best friends from college

Pay down my credit card debt so I can start saving for a house

Speak at a public event in the next year

Take an improv comedy class

Take a class in coding/build a mobile app

GOALS BRAINSTORM

What are some of my goals for the next three months?

_____

01

_____

02

_____

03

_____

04

_____

05

06

07

08

09

10

BEGIN WITH
THE END
IN MIND.

NARROWING MY FOCUS

Here are the top four goals I will work on over the next three months:

_____

01

_____

02

_____

03

_____

04

HoW To BREAK
YOUR GOALS
INTO TINY LITTLE STEPS

Setting EPIC goals is the first step. The easiest way to stay on track is to break a bigger goal into smaller steps.

This helps you plan for any potential road blocks and gives that extra spike of dopamine as you start to cross things off the list.

Continuing with the example from the previous pages, in order to cook three times a week, you have to start with smaller goals:

- Research healthy recipes
- Make a shopping list
- Buy groceries
- Prep ingredients in the morning before work
- Cook the meal

By breaking down the smaller steps in detail, you can slowly start checking things off the list.

Once you start ticking tiny tasks off your list, your confidence will continue to grow and the momentum will propel you closer and closer to achieving your goals.

PLANNING IS ONLY THE FIRST STEP—
THEN YOU HAVE TO DO THE WORK.

GOAL:

ACTION STEPS:

_____

_____

_____

_____

_____

_____

_____

_____

_____

_____

_____

_____

GOAL:

ACTION STEPS:

GOAL:

ACTION STEPS:

_____

_____

_____

_____

_____

_____

_____

_____

_____

_____

_____

GOAL:

ACTION STEPS:

_____

_____

_____

_____

_____

_____

_____

_____

_____

_____

_____

CELEBRATE THE WINS

Congratulations! You completed the workbook. Your hard work deserves a pat on the back.

I hope that this book has helped you learn about yourself and the things that you want to achieve. Sit in this moment of empowerment and know that you can make your dreams become reality.

It's no easy feat to take the time and energy to invest in building your ideal life. But you have the courage and the grit to make it happen.

In case no one told you yet today: You are talented, intelligent, and capable. You were uniquely designed to make a meaningful impact in the world. But it's your responsibility to find the strength to build the life you want to lead. That takes daily decisions to honor your future self by doing the hard work today. I believe in you and the magic you are destined to create.

Before we say goodbye, I want to remind you of a few important things.

1. You are worthy. Of love. Of joy. Of peace. Of every opportunity you can think of for yourself. Your worthiness is not contingent on anything. You were born worthy. So forgive yourself for all those little (and large) mistakes you made along the way. Move forward believing that you deserve the best life you can imagine. Because you do.

2. You don't need to fix yourself. You're not broken. But hopefully with the right set of tools, you can learn to better cope with the daily challenges of life.

3. Therapy is miraculous. It literally changed my life, and it can do the same for you. While reading, prayer, eating to feel good, and daily mindful movement are also a part of my wellness journey, therapy is what helped me actually start to change my life. If you've considered going to therapy, here's another gentle nudge to give it a try. It's difficult, but it's also liberating. I want you to feel the freedom of accepting and loving yourself wholeheartedly! A licensed professional can help in ways you cannot always do on your own. So don't wait any longer!

ABOUT THE AUTHOR

JUSTIN SHIELS has always been compelled by the power of words and pictures to change hearts and minds. He received his BFA in graphic design from Loyola University New Orleans and his masters in arts administration from the University of New Orleans. His creative career has led him down many paths, working in advertising and tech, launching a magazine, and starting a conference. But his journey has always connected him back to making people feel things. Now, as a writer, illustrator, and speaker, Justin creates inspirational content for curious and thoughtful people. He developed the workbook he always needed—something to help him design the life he wanted to live.

It was scary and hard and often made him feel like a complete fraud. But he did it because it was the work he was supposed to be doing.

What big, scary thing should you be doing right now?

The journey doesn't have to end here. If you'd like to stay connected, I encourage you to sign up for my weekly email at **soCurious.co**. Every issue includes an inspirational message, some recommendations, and original illustration.

It feels like a warm hug from an old friend.